Kate Donachie is a Scottish solicitor with more than 20 years' experience representing a variety of clients in personal injury and other civil actions. She is past Chair of the Forum of Insurance Lawyers in Scotland, and of the Forum's large loss sector focus team. She was involved in scrutiny of the Civil Litigation (Expenses and Group Proceedings) Act when it was passing through the Scottish Parliament and gave evidence to the Scottish Parliament's Justice Committee in relation to the Damages (Investment Returns and Periodical Payments) (Scotland) Act.

She has been recognised her for her intuitive and thorough approach to claims and her common-sense way of solving problems. She has presented to the Law Society of Scotland Personal Injury Conference on a number of occasions and regularly presents at client and public events. She is regularly published in the insurance trade, and the general press in relation to issues pertinent to civil litigation in Scotland.

A Practical Guide to Fraudulent and Exaggerated Personal Injury Claims in Scotland

A Practical Guide to Fraudulent and Exaggerated Personal Injury Claims in Scotland

Kate Donachie LLB (Hons) Dip LP, NP.

Law Brief Publishing

Published 2025 by Law Brief Publishing, an imprint of Law Brief Publishing Ltd
30 The Parks
Minehead
Somerset
TA24 8BT

www.lawbriefpublishing.com

Paperback: 978-1-916698-80-2

PREFACE

This book arises from what seems to be a real lack of clarity and understanding around what fraud is in the civil context, and how the Scottish procedure can and should be used to manage fraud. I hope that it is a useful and interesting text which allows for the effective practical navigation of these cases. I am grateful to my family and colleagues for the help and encouragement they gave me while the book was being written. The law is correct as at 31st December 2024.

Kate Donachie
January 2025

CONTENTS

INTRODUCTION

Allegations of fraud or fraudulent exaggeration arise relatively frequently in Scottish personal injury cases. However, without a dedicated procedure, or any specific rules, it can be difficult for practitioners to know how such allegations should be managed.

The position in Scotland is perhaps confused because there is specific legislative provision in England and Wales for the management of fraudulent personal injury claims. This can give rise to the temptation to view the management of Scottish fraudulent claims through the prism of that framework, rather than understanding and relying upon the Scottish system of civil litigation.

The Scottish system offers various means by which fraudulent behaviour can be challenged, and by which allegations of fraud can be resisted. This book seeks to provide a comprehensive practical guide to managing fraud in Scottish personal injury actions. It also considers the impact of QOCS on the determination and definition of fraud in personal injury actions.

Knowing and understanding the Scottish definition of fraud is crucial to successfully navigating potentially fraudulent cases; it is the thread that connects all of the practical aspects considered in the book and is therefore the starting point.

Thereafter the book considers whether the Scottish courts have the power to dismiss a claim which has a meritorious component, on the basis that the pursuer has acted so fraudulently that they should be denied even the genuine part of their claim. This is an issue which perhaps suffers most from confusion with the approach in England and Wales, and it is important to understand the powers of the Scottish courts and the circumstances in which those powers have previously been exercised. The decisive factor for the Scottish courts is not the gravity of the pursuer's dishonesty, but rather the impact that the dishonesty has had on the court's ability to fairly determine the issues between the parties; this is therefore a preliminary measure, a decision to be made before proof.

Where it is not possible to have the entire claim dismissed on the basis that the pursuer's fraudulent behaviour has frustrated a fair trial, there are other ways in which the claim can be defended. The pursuer, and their witnesses' credibility and reliability can be challenged, allowing a submission that their evidence should not be taken into account by the decision maker. Similarly, where the pursuer's behaviour has precluded the necessary evidence being presented to court, there can be a submission that the pursuer has failed to adequately prove the case. The rules and procedures surrounding such arguments, and the distinction between credibility and reliability are explored and explained.

There are of course some cases which are entirely fraudulent and the evidential onus and weight for that are considered along with the procedural requirements and exceptions. The significance of the particular findings in fact made after proof is highlighted.

Finally, the book explores the impact of QOCS, and the approach taken to date in relation to the definition of "fraudulent misrepresentation" along with the procedural requirements for bringing such an argument.

CHAPTER ONE

THE SCOTTISH DEFINITION OF FRAUD

The classic definition of fraud is relevant to all aspects of fraud in personal injury actions. It is therefore important to understand the definition and what is required to establish fraud in Scotland.

John Erskine [Inst, III,I,16] and George Joseph Bell [Principles, para 13], two of Scotland's institutional writers defined fraud as "*a machination or contrivance to deceive*".

The definition confirms the intentional element necessary for fraud, a machination is *"a complicated and secret plan to get power or control or to gain an advantage"* [Collins, 2020] similarly, a contrivance is *"the act of intentionally arranging for something to happen by clever planning, or something that is arranged in this way"* [Collins, 2020].

This definition is however viewed as expansive in that it allows for any number of methods or schemes by which to achieve the deception.

The definition of criminal fraud in Scotland

Before moving on to consider fraud in the context of civil actions, it is worthwhile setting out the definition and requirements of the crime of fraud in Scotland. This is important because it provides some insight into the way in which fraud is viewed in civil disputes, and the underlying principles are relevant in both criminal and civil contexts.

The law in Scotland on this point differs to that in England and Wales. In Scotland, criminal fraud is a common law offence, it is not defined in legislation. This contrasts with the position in England and Wales, where fraud is defined by the **Fraud Act 2006**.

In order for an offence of fraud to have been committed in Scotland, three elements must be proven, that the accused has made a false pretence, that there has been a practical result, and that the practical result was brought about by the false pretence.

False pretence

This can be express, [*Stueurt v Macpherson* 1918 SC JC 96 97] friends cheating together at cards asserting that they didn't know each other, or implied, [*James Paton* (1858) 3 Irvine 208] a farmer modifying his cattle to improve their prospects in acattle show by pumping them with air to make them seem larger. It can also be staying silent where there is an obligation to speak up, this arises in certain financial transactions, for example failing to disclose material facts when obtaining loans or insurance. [*Buchmann v Normand* 1994 SCCR 929]

The crucial element is intent. Changing your mind, or not paying debts is unlikely to satisfy the requirement. However, stating an intent which you know to be untrue at the time, with the intention of achieving some beneficial result will be. [*Richards v HM Advocate* 1971 JC 29 – pretending that houses would be used as private residential homes in order to induce sale]

Practical effect

This was most recently considered in the case of ***Whyte v HM Advocate*** [2017 J.C. 262]. It arose in the prosecution of an individual accused of fraudulently acquiring a Scottish Football club. It was argued on behalf of the accused that as there had not been any actual loss, the charges against him were irrelevant. That argument was rejected at first instance, because the court considered itself bound by ***Adcock v Archibald*** [1925 JC 58], long considered to provide the authoritative approach to the issue. In that decision, the Lord Justice General (Clyde) said that it was not necessary to prove a loss and that it was instead sufficient to show that fraud had achieved *"any definite practical result"*. Adcock was a miner who switched tags on bags of coal, to make it appear that he had mined the coal in the bag when it had in fact been another miner. However, both miners failed to mine sufficient coal to earn the minimum wage, and the employer was bound to make up both miners' pay to minimum wage. The miner's dishonesty had not therefore brought him any gain. However, the court held it sufficient that the employer had attributed the bag of coal to Adcock, as it had been *"induced by false pretences to do what they would otherwise not have done"*

The accused appealed on the basis that ***Adcock*** was wrongly decided, and that it was necessary for the "dupe" to have suffered some prejudice as a result of the fraud, Hearing the appeal in The High Court of Justiciary, Lady Dorrian, Lord Justice Clerk, rejected with reference to the line of authority preceding ***Adcock*** [*HMA v Smith* (1893) 1 Adam 6; Turnbull v Stewart (1898) 25R (J) 78 and *Hood v Young* June 10 1853, 1 Irv 236.] the appellant's argument and affirmed the ***Adcock*** decision. She found that, changes in commercial practice notwithstanding, it remained sufficient to demonstrate that there had been a practical impact as a result of the fraud, it was not necessary to show any loss. Lady Dorrian commented that "*the principle in Adcock has the virtue of being clear, objective, sufficiently* *flexible to address changing commercial situations, and which apparently has worked successfully for over 90 years*" [per Lady Dorrian para 150]

Significantly Lady Dorrian rejected the argument that fraud was essentially a crime against property. She held, following, ***Adcock***, that fraud is a crime of dishonesty, there need be no impact on property for the crime to be complete.

Causal connection

As already noted, the crime is committed when someone is induced by false pretences to do what they would not otherwise have done. If there is no practical result, the crime is not committed. Similarly, if it is shown that the practical result would have occurred even in the absence of the false representation, the crime is not committed.

However, attempted fraud is a crime in Scotland. To prove that crime, it is necessary to show that had the deception been successful, there would have been a practical result.

Intention

In ***Whyte*** Lady Dorrian observed that the requirement for a practical result, and a causal connection between that and the dishonesty, served as "*important safeguards against the criminalisation of innocent behaviour, or mere lies.*"

There is a further component which serves the same purpose, intention; there is no crime of fraud in Scotland unless the accused, knew the representation was false, and intended to bring about the practical result, careless or inadvertent dishonesty will not be fraud.

This requirement and safeguard is reflected in Erskine's definition of fraud, "*a machination or contrivance to deceive* [Inst, III,I,16] because, in order to be a machination or a contrivance, the behaviour must involve a deliberate plan or plot, and not something which is inadvertent or opportunistic.

Definition of fraudulent representation in Scottish civil law

Although it is recognised that fraudulent behaviour may take any number of forms, in civil law, as in criminal, it must be deliberate "*the mere fact of the inaccuracy of the statement ought not to be pressed into constituting a liability which appears to me not to exist.*" [*Derry v Peek* (1889) 14 App. Cas 337) per Lord Halsbury at 344].

The judgement of Lord Hershell in ***Derry*** in which he said, *"Fraud is proved when it is shown that a false representation has been made (1) knowingly, or (2) without belief in its truth, or (3) recklessly, careless whether it be true or false."*[374] was accepted as reflecting the Scottish law by the House of Lords in ***Robinson v National Bank of Scotland*** [1916 SC (H.L.) 154] where it was found that a representation which was inaccurate and careless, but not dishonest, was not fraudulent. Indeed, Earl Loreburn expressed his hope that the term fraud would only be applied in circumstances where there was *"moral delinquency"* [155]. Viscount Haldane [at 157] emphasised that there was no "*duty to be careful*" and with reference to Derry, commented that the duty was one of "*common honesty*".

It is to be noted that these observations apply in relation to a finding of fraud generally. Other duties may be imposed by way of the particular relationship between the parties. In such circumstances, for example, where there is a fiduciary relationship, silence could amount to a fraudulent misrepresentation, essentially, dishonesty by "*concealment*" [*Adams v R* [1995] 1 WLR 52 (HL), Lord Jauncey of Tullichettle at 65.].

An inaccurate but honestly made representation will not be fraud, there must be "*actual dishonesty*". [McBryde on Contract 3rd Edition para 4-12].

Although there is arguably a personal element to whether a representation was honestly made, because someone may have believed the statement to be true on the basis of their knowledge at the time, honesty itself is an objective standard [*Starglade Properties Ltd v Nash* [2010] EWCA Civ 1314 , Chancellor (Morritt) at paragraph 32.]. This reflects the risk that a different approach would allow honesty to be considered as on "*an optional scale, with higher or lower values according to the moral standards of each individual*" [*Royal Brunei Airlines v Tan* [1995] 2 AC 278 per Lord Nicholls of Birkenhead p 389 C-F]. It will not be relevant that the person making the misrepresentation thought it was "*honest enough*" or not "*materially untrue*". The test is whether "*by ordinary standards a defendant's mental state would be characterised as dishonest*" [*Barlow Clowes Ltd v Eurotrust ltd* [2006] 1WLR 1476 at para 10].

However, even although the standard is objective, when considering whether a representation was made honestly, the court should take into account everything known by the person at the time and the assessment should also take account of their own experience and intelligence [*Royal Brunei Airlines v Tan* [1995] 2 AC 278 at p391B].

Requirement of a practical outcome

Proof that the misrepresentation has brought about a practical outcome is also necessary to establish fraud in the civil context. It is not sufficient simply to show that someone has been deliberately dishonest, the dishonesty must have been intended to, and has, precipitated some action, for example that the target would enter into a transaction or make an investment which when they would not have done so in the absence of the misrepresentation. [*Kidd v Paull & Williamson LLP* [2017] CSOH 16].

In order to prove loss arising from the fraud, it is necessary to show that the misrepresentation materially influenced the victim's decision to take the action. While there is a presumption in favour of materiality, and it is sufficient for the misrepresentation to be "*an inducing*" and not the *"sole"* cause [*Zurich Insurance Co Plc v Hayward* [2016] UKSC 48 per Lord Clarke of Stone-Cum-Ebony JSC at156]. The pleadings must contain an averment to the effect that there was a connection between the misrepresentation and the decision to proceed [*Kidd v Paull & Williamson LLP* [2017] CSOH 16].

The victim need not actually believe that the misrepresentation is true, but the absence of such a belief will make it more difficult to prove that they were induced to do something. It might be possible, for example, in the context of a personal injury claim, to show that although the victim did not entirely believe the misrepresentation, they honestly believed that the court would [*Zurich Insurance Co Plc v Hayward* [2016] UKSC 48]. This is consistent with the requirement that the misrepresentation induced the victim to do something they would not otherwise have done; there is no requirement that the victim was actually fooled.

Summary

The key components of fraud in Scotland are that the dishonesty was deliberate, and that there was an intention to use the dishonesty to achieve a practical effect.

It is clear that fraud will not arise where someone has said something which is inaccurate, but which they genuinely believed to be true. Similarly, there will not be fraud unless the dishonesty was intended to achieve a particular result.

In deciding whether a personal injury claim, or elements of the claim, are fraudulent, these are the principles which will be applied by the court, and they can be seen running through all of the various circumstances in which the issue arises.

CHAPTER TWO

CIVIL FRAUD IN SCOTLAND – THE POWER TO DISMISS AN ACTION

The position in England Wales – Fundamental Dishonesty

In England and Wales, a case which reaches the threshold of "Fundamental Dishonesty" must be dismissed in its entirety, including any elements of the claim which are genuine. This rule was introduced by s57 of **Criminal Justice and Courts Act 2015**. It is for the defendant to argue and prove fundamental dishonesty. S57 changed the previous position where the court could only dispose of that part of the claim which was dishonest [for example *Summers v Fairclough Homes* [2012] 1 WLR].

There is an exception in terms of S57(2) whereby the court need not dismiss the entire claim where, were it to do so, "*the claimant would suffer substantial injustice*". However, decisions since 2015 have demonstrated that the bar is very high for the application of the exception, and in the vast majority of cases, the full claim will be dismissed where the threshold of fundamental dishonesty is reached.

What is required to reach the threshold is relatively settled. The dishonesty must go to the "*root of*" at least a "*substantial*" part of the claim [*Howlett v Davies* [2017] EWCA Civ 1696 and *Pegg v Webb* [2020] EWHC 2095 (QB)] or "*substantially affect the claim*" [*London Organising Committee of the Olympic and Paralympic Games v Sinfield* [2018] EWHC 51 (QB)]. Where a claimant was dishonest about how he came to suffer an injury, that did not amount to fundamental dishonesty in a claim which related to clinical negligence.

[*Cojanu v Essex Partnership University NHS Trust* [2022] EWHC 197 (QB)].

The position in Scotland

By contrast, fundamental dishonesty is not a recognised concept in Scottish civil litigation, and there is no specific procedure for the management or disposal of cases in which fraud is alleged. This can lead to uncertainty and unpredictability when attempting to decide strategy for such a case.

One option, which is considered in this chapter, is to ask the court to exercise its inherent power to dismiss an entire claim on the basis that the pursuer's behaviour is sufficiently fraudulent, or alternatively, to argue that the case should be dismissed because the pursuer's dishonesty amounts to an abuse of process. To be clear, this approach would involve the court disposing of elements of the pursuer's case which might be genuine, notwithstanding dishonesty in relation to other elements of the claim.

However, although it is accepted that the Scottish Courts do have this power, what limited authority there is, makes it clear that the power is considered a "*drastic*" [*Shetland Sea Farms Ltd v Assuranceforeningen Skuld*, 2004 SLT 30 2001] one, and it will be exercised only sparingly.

It is important for practitioners to understand the underlying rationale for courts' exercise of this power in the past, and therefore how to approach any argument that a case should be dismissed because it is fraudulent when it arises in practice.

What is an inherent power?

An inherent power is one which is not set out explicitly in statute, nor necessarily found in previous decisions of the court, or the court rules [*Tonner v Reiach and Hall* 2008 SC 1] but one which is an integral part of the court's authority to fulfil its function. Erskine recognised this inherent power [Institutes 1-2-8] "*every power is understood to be conferred without which the jurisdiction cannot be explicated*" and Lord Justice- General Emslie, delivering the decision of the court in ***Cordiner Ptr*** [1973 JC 16 at (p18)] observed that *"Both the Court of Session and this Court [High Court] have an inherent and necessary jurisdiction to take effective action to vindicate their authority and preserve the due and impartial administration of justice"*.

This power has not been universally accepted without challenge, it was argued relatively recently that the Court of Session is a statutory court and so therefore does not possess the power [*Hepburn v Royal Alexandria Hospital* 2011 SC 20] however that argument was rejected. It was also observed that this power, which was conferred on the Court of Session by the **College of Justice Act 1540**, had previously been reserved to the king, which perhaps serves to underline its importance and strength.

The more contentious question is rather, when, and in what way, will the court exercise the power. The difficulty with which the exercise of the power can be justified is seen in its description as "*An option of last resort*" [*Tonner v Reiach and Hall* 2008 SC 1 at para 123]. It has also been emphasised that the power does not simply allow a Division or judge of the court to *"do what it or he considers ought to be in done in a given case in accordance with that Division's or judge's notion of what justice requires"* [*Hepburn v Royal Alexandria Hospital* 2011 SC 20 per Lord Carloway para 54]. As more fully explained below, the power has a practical function and can only be exercised in order to allow the court to "*do whatever is necessary to discharge the whole of its responsibilities"* [*Hall v Associated Newspapers Ltd* [1979 JC 1] per Lord Justice General Emslie at page 9].

What is the purpose of the power?

By necessity, this is not a power which can be delineated or exhaustively defined. It can be wide ranging; it has been confirmed that the power to sanction can extend beyond the conduct of court proceedings, and beyond the parties engaged in the court process. For example, a sanction was imposed on a newspaper for publishing details of murder investigation after the point at which the accused had been detained by the police, but before he had been charged with the offence or committed for trial; the court held that an accused was "*under the protection of the court*" from the point they were arrested. [*Hall v Associated Newspapers Ltd* [1979 JC 1]]. In the civil context the power is unlikely to extend beyond the commencement of the action and has been described as beginning at the point the initial writ or summons is served [Ibid p10]. The key function of the exercise of the power in Hall, was characterised as being to protect a party's right to *"a fair and impartial trial*" and to prevent prejudice to the proceedings.

The power can be exercised to dismiss civil actions in a variety of circumstances. It is accepted that the court can dismiss an action for want of insistence [*Tonner v Reiach and Hall* 2008 SC 1 and *Hepburn v Royal Alexandria Hospital* 2011 SC 20]. However, here too, the power is not exercised as a punishment, but rather to prevent procedural unfairness. Where a fair trial is still possible, notwithstanding unreasonable delay, the action should not be dismissed [*Hepburn v Royal Alexandria Hospital* 2011 SC 20].

It has been suggested that the ability to hold a fair trial, while a significant consideration, is not determinative [*Grubb v Finlay* [2018] CSIH 29, per Lord Carolway para 34] however while it might not be strictly necessary to show that a fair trial is not possible, the determinative factor appears to be, at least, whether the behaviour complained of gives rise to the risk more widely that *"justice cannot be done"* [*Hepburn v Royal Alexandria Hospital* 2011 SC 20 per Lord Reed para [51]]. That is, the delay, contempt of court or abuse of process, must have a practical effect on the court's function. [*Moore v Scottish Daily Record and Sunday Mail* 2009 SC 178, at para 13]. It has been proposed that the impact on the court's ability to reach a just decision need not be on the immediate case; dismissal could perhaps be justified where to allow one action to proceed would interfere with the administration of justice in another. [*Hepburn v Royal Alexandria Hospital* 2011 SC 20 per Lord Reed para [50]]. However there have been no decisions in which this type of consideration was found sufficient to justify dismissal.

The relevance of the requirement for this practical impact is that where the "*court cannot be satisfied that a just determination of the dispute remains possible...it cannot otherwise fulfil its constitutional function as a court of justice.*" [*Hepburn v Royal Alexandria Hospital* 2011 SC 20 per Lord Reed para [47]]. Accordingly, the power to dismiss a case in such circumstances is integral to the court's fundamental purpose.

Dismissal for fraud

While it is true that the power could be exercised to dismiss a case where the pursuer has been dishonest or has conducted the proceedings fraudulently, bare proof of fraud or dishonesty will not be sufficient to dismiss an action in its entirety [*Grubb v Finlay* [2018] CSIH 29]. The courts will not deny a pursuer a "*well founded claim*" and will uphold the *"general right of every litigant to pursue his case to judgment"* [*Shetland Sea Farms Ltd v Assuranceforeningen Skuld,* 2004 SLT 30 2001 per Lord Gill para 143]

As noted, it has been suggested that dismissal could be justified with reference to the administration of justice beyond the immediate action, however, the decisions in which dismissal has been considered have specified the requirement for the fraud to prevent the ability of the court to reach a fair disposal of the dispute at hand. For example, where key documents had been lost by the pursuer and the defender could no longer rely on those documents as evidence of the pursuer's previous dishonesty [*Levison v Jewish Chronicle* 1924 SLT 755]. It was observed that, the fraud must have a practical effect "*calculated to prejudice materially the interests of the defenders*" [Ibid, per Lord Ashmore 759].

Where the fraud was in the past and would not impede a fair determination of the dispute in the future, dismissal was not justified [*Shetland Sea Farms Ltd v Assuranceforeningen Skuld*, 2004 SLT 30 2001, per Lord Gill para 146]. In order to justify exercise of the power, it was necessary both that the pursuer was guilty of abuse of process, and that this behaviour made a fair trial impossible [Ibid, per Lord Gill para 146]. That is, the dismissal is not justified solely as a punishment for abuse of process, the abuse of process must have frustrated the court's ability to fulfil its purpose. It is clear that the loss of an otherwise potentially good case cannot be inflicted on a pursuer as "*judicial retaliation for affront to the court*" [Ibid].

In his 2016 speech, ***Lies, damned lies: Abuse of process and the dishonest litigant*** [1 The Rt Hon Lord Reed 26 October 2012, [https://www.supremecourt.uk/docs/speech-121026.pdf] Lord Reed gives the fifth Annual Lecture at the Centre for Commercial Law, University of Edinburgh (PDF)] Lord Reed argued that the courts should be more willing to dismiss cases for what he described as abuse of process, and where the impact was not on the other party to the dispute, nor on the ability to hold a fair trial, but more widely on the ability of the court system to function. Lord Reed highlighted the fact that although a fair trial might ultimately be possible, as was the position in the subsequent case of ***Grubb***, and in ***Summers***, gross and fraudulent exaggeration by a pursuer has a cost in terms of court and other resources. He suggested that the interests of justice can be conceived as *"encompassing the wider public interest in the administration of justice"*.

Lord Reed also drew a parallel with the dismissal of cases for a failure to comply with the rules of court [*Brogan v O'Rourke* 2005 SLT 29] where it was noted (by Lord Reed) that *"The interests of justice are not well served by an approach which too readily excuses failures to comply with those rules"*. [Ibid, para 33]

Lord Reed's prediction, or least hope, that the Scottish courts might be more willing to dismiss cases even where a fair trial remained possible, has not been realised. As noted, in the subsequent case of ***Grubb***, the Inner House held that it could not dismiss the claim in its entirely because to do so would be to deprive the pursuer of the genuine portion of his claim.

However, it is worth noting that in ***Grubb***, although the pursuer was found to have been dishonest on a number of points, the Lord Ordinary, was able to find independent evidence to support many elements of the claim. The pursuer's medical experts advised that it would not have been possible for the pursuer to falsify his presentation nor the symptoms apparent at examination. In addition, although symptoms beyond 12 months could not be attributed (as claimed by the pursuer) to the accident, the Lord Ordinary did not find that the pursuer's erroneous attribution was dishonest, or fraudulent. Lord Carloway was also critical of the point at which the defender made the motion for dismissal.

However, Lord Carloway's decision makes it plain that the concept of fundamental dishonesty as provided for in the 2015 Act has not been incorporated into Scottish Law. Lord Carloway concludes that the pursuer in ***Grubb*** was not fundamentally dishonest because his case was accepted as genuine to the extent that he was in an accident, that it was of the nature he described, and that he suffered injury. Lord Carloway describes the pursuer's claim as a "*good claim*". The pursuer was found to have been deliberately dishonest on a number of points and was awarded £7,321.32, having claimed £500,000.

The contrast between the approach in Scotland and England and Wales can be highlighted to some extent by comparing the outcome in Grubb to that in ***Pinkus v Direct Line* [2018] EWHC 1671 (AB)**. In the latter case the claimant was found to be fundamentally dishonest, and his entire claim was dismissed. The court found that the claimant had exaggerated the gravity of the accident, his injuries and their effect on him to an egregious extent. The judge provided, as required by the 2015 Act, that in the absence of the dishonesty, he would have awarded the claimant £4,729. His claim had initially been for more than £1million but he had reduced the figure and was seeking to a little under £1million shortly before trial.

Summary

It is important to bear in mind that where proof has taken place, the argument that the entire case should be dismissed, notwithstanding a finding that there has been some genuine loss as a consequence of the defender's fault, is not consistent with the requirement that the dishonesty must preclude a fair trial.

Although it has been suggested that the Scottish courts have the power to dismiss a case in which a fair trial could be held, there are no cases in which that has been the outcome. Even on that wider approach, it would be necessary to show that the dishonesty had some further reaching impact on the administration of justice.

At present, it seems unlikely, in the absence of legislative change, that the approach taken by the Scottish courts to this issue will change.

CHAPTER THREE

CHALLENGES TO THE CREDIBILITY AND RELIABILITY OF WITNESSES

Chapter two considered whether it was competent for a Scottish court to dismiss a case in its entirety, before proof, on the basis that the pursuer had been dishonest.

In the only Scottish cases [*Shetland Sea Farms Ltd v Assuranceforeningen Skuld,* 2004 SLT 30 2001 and *Levison v Jewish Chronicle* 1924 SLT 755] to have explicitly considered dismissal of an entire (partially good) action before proof on the basis that the pursuer had been dishonest, the test imposed by the court was whether the pursuer's actions either rendered a fair trial impossible, or significantly reduced the possibility of a fair trial. Despite some suggestion that there may be alternative circumstances in which the Scottish courts could dismiss a case before proof, the authorities to date indicate that this is unlikely.

However, where the pursuer has been dishonest to the extent of introducing false heads of loss or exaggerating genuine losses, it may be possible to persuade the court to restrict the extent, or remove aspects, of the pursuer's claim because they have been presented fraudulently. This requires an evidential hearing and would generally be the subject of submissions at the conclusion of proof. As discussed in Chapter Two, in England and Wales an entire claim will be dismissed, including any genuine elements, if the behaviour is found to constitute fundamental dishonesty. In Scotland, only the fraudulent, or unproven elements will be removed; it is not necessary to prove that the entire claim is fraudulent, nor to prove that the case has reached any overall threshold of dishonesty.

In England and Wales there are quite specific pleadings required to support an argument that the claimant is fundamentally dishonest. In Scotland, there are specific requirements for pleadings to support an assertion of fraud where it is plead as a substantive defence, or in support of the claim [*Royal Bank of Scotland v Holmes* 1999 S.L.T. 563 and *Leander CB Consultants Limited T/A Leandor Advisors v Bogside Investments Limited, Alan Carson Mcleish* [2023] CSOH 26].

However, where it is argued instead that the claim or elements of the claim itself are fraudulently presented and should be rejected, it is really the pursuer's credibility and reliability which are being attacked. The requirements for such arguments are not as prescriptive as in other contexts.

This chapter considers how to approach arguments about witnesses' credibility and reliability in personal injury actions.

Sufficiency of single witness evidence

In Scottish criminal cases it is necessary for evidence to be corroborated, i.e. a fact must have two sources of evidence in order for it to be considered proven. This was also previously required in civil cases; however, **S9(2)** of the **Law Reform (Miscellaneous Provisions) (Scotland) Act 1968** abolished the requirement for corroboration in civil cases. Although S9 was later repealed by **S1(1) Civil Evidence (Scotland) Act 1988** the subsequent legislation also provides that a court or jury can find a fact proven even if the evidence is not corroborated.

S2 of the **1988 Act** abolished the hearsay rule and accordingly it is competent to lead what could be considered "second hand evidence" although such evidence is likely to be afforded less weight than that provided by the primary witness.

For current purposes it is important to note that the pursuer's evidence need not be corroborated in order to be considered sufficient to prove their case. This can become an issue where the pursuer's evidence is contradicted, but if the evidence is sufficiently persuasive it is open to the court to prefer the evidence of a single witness over evidence from other sources. [*L v L* 1997 SCLR 866 per Lord Coulsfield at 876]

Credibility and reliability

If a witness gives evidence, it can be submitted that the evidence should be disregarded on the basis that it is not credible or reliable. In order to consider how to make and respond to such challenges, it is helpful first to consider the concepts and what they mean.

Credibility is essentially the truthfulness of a witness, and arguably there is a necessarily deliberate component to credibility; if someone's evidence is considered incredible then, by implication, they are aware that the evidence is not truthful.

In contrast, reliability concerns the quality of the evidence, rather than the person who provides the evidence. A witness can be considered entirely truthful by the court, but their evidence discounted nonetheless for being inaccurate. In ***Prescott v University of St Andrews*** [2016] CSOH 3, the pursuer gave detailed evidence of his attendance in the University library at times when there would have been asbestos in the atmosphere. However, although accepting that the pursuer was not seeking to mislead the court, Lord Pentland concluded that the pursuer's evidence was incorrect. Significantly Lord Pentland described the process of remembering events from long ago as being of a "*reconstructive nature*" and highlighted that this aspect was "*largely unconscious*" thus emphasising the fact that deliberate deception is not necessary for a finding of unreliability. [Ibid at 43]

Notwithstanding the distinction between these two concepts, they are often bundled together, both by those seeking to attack a witness' evidence and by the court adjudicating on the point. However, in making or meeting a challenge to a witnesses' evidence it is useful to understand what is being alleged, and whether it is sufficient to undermine some or all of the witnesses' evidence.

For example, if a witness gives evidence on one point which is inadvertently inconsistent with other evidence, that should not necessarily taint their evidence on other points. However, if a witness has deliberately provided information which is inaccurate, then there would be some force in the argument that the witness' evidence on other points should be considered in light of their willingness to deliberately provide false evidence.

Whether there has been deliberate dishonesty is also relevant to a positive finding that the pursuer has been fraudulent in their presentation of their case, considered in Chapter 4.

How is a witness' evidence tested for credibility and reliability?

This is ultimately a matter for the court, there are no firm rules on what will or will not, render a witness credible or reliable. Indeed, given the nature of the exercise, the application of standard rules has not been considered beneficial, "*it is for the court to assess all of the evidence which is led in a case and to determine its weight, a difficult but very practical exercise which calls for the application of the judge's or jury's store of wisdom and common sense Unfortunately rules of law are not likely to assist them in performing their task. For that reasons such rules should obtrude as little as possible into the process" [LvL* 1997 SCLR 866 at 871 Per Lord Roger at E].

There are however factors which are generally considered relevant by the court when weighing the credibility and reliability of a witness.

Demeanour

Where credibility is an issue, the demeanour of the witness giving evidence can be relevant, albeit not the decisive factor [*Onassis v Vergottis* [1968] 2 Lloyd's Rep 403 *Wetton (as Liquidator of Mumtaz Properties)* v *Ahmed and Others* [2011] EWCA Civ 610 and *McLeod's Legal Representatives v Highland Health Board* [2016] CSIH25 Per Lord Brodie at 95].

A witnesses' demeanour can include the way in which answers are given for example an inability to give a "*simple answer to a simple question*" [*Shanley v Clydesdale Bank PLC* [2019] CSOH 75 at 33] "*long winded*" responses and appearing to "*struggle in thinking*" before answering [*Leander CB Consultants Limited T/A Leandor Advisors v Bogside Investments Limited, Alan Carson Mcleish* [2024] CSOH 09 at para 12]. It can also include providing information not requested, such as their location at the point of the accident when they had simply been asked where they were holidaying at the time of the accident and agreeing to contradictory statements about their intended destination [*Gilmour v Linea Directa Aseguradora Sa Compania De Seguros Y Reaseguros* [2017] SC EDIN 81 p20].

A demeanour which contradicts evidence about the impact of an event, and which differs over the course of the hearing can be persuasive of dishonesty, for example a *"robust, combative and feisty performance*" which contrasted with both the "*account and presentation*" in chief was considered evidence of a "*very considerable degree of exaggeration*" on the pursuer's part [*Ormsby v Chief Constable of Strathclyde Police* [2008] CSOH 143 at para 96].

As noted, poor demeanour alone is unlikely to be sufficient to undermine a witnesses' credibility, but it will be considered a relevant factor to be weighed in the balance, and it is something to which the court can look for reassurance if the evidence has been put in question [*L v L* 1997 SCLR 866 per Lord Rodger 874]. Positive signs include the witness admitting when they are uncertain about something they have been asked [*Elizabeth Fairley v Edinburgh Trams* [2019] CSOH 50 at p 171].

Inconsistency with other evidence

Where evidence given by a witness is contradicted by other evidence presented in the case then it will be necessary to consider the credibility and reliability of each piece of evidence given by that witness. Where the evidence which contradicts the witness is considered credible, then it may be difficult for the court to find that the witness' evidence is accurate [*Leander CB Consultants Limited T/A Leandor Advisors v Bogside Investments Limited, Alan Carson Mcleish* [2024] CSOH 09 at para 10]. Similar issues can arise where the contradictory evidence has been given by another witness whose evidence has been considered credible and reliable by the court, and who is considered disinterested in the outcome of the case [*Gilmour v Linea Directa Aseguradora Sa Compania De Seguros Y Reaseguros* [2017] SC EDIN 81].

Inconsistency with witness' own evidence – prior inconsistent statement

Where a witness has previously provided evidence which contradicts the evidence given at proof, that previous evidence can be put to the witness in order to challenge their credibility or reliability. An inconsistency can be sufficient to establish that the witness is neither credible nor reliable *[Gilmour v Linea Directa Aseguradora Sa Compania De Seguros Y Reaseguros* [2017] SC EDIN 81 and *Hill v Angus Council* [2023] SAC 9(Civ) 15].

Putting a prior inconsistent statement to a witness, or party to the action, is not considered an ambush because the information is *"well known*" to the witness *[Robertson v Anderson* 2014 SLT 709 at 67].

Inherent improbability of evidence and inconsistency with judicial knowledge.

Even where there is no positive evidence of an alternative scenario the court may reject a witness' evidence on the basis that it is inherently unlikely to be true. For example, where a witness described having telephone numbers for two individuals stored in his mobile telephone, but denied knowing their names, and where the witness failed to call his own insurance company after an accident which he described as having caused "*substantial damage*" to his vehicle [*Khan v AXA Insurance PLC* [2024] SC EDIN18 at Para 101].

Similarly, the witness' evidence that he had delayed making a claim because he was too busy at University was found incredible on the basis that the accident had taken place in July, and so therefore during a holiday period and that the claim had ultimately been intimated during term time, [Ibid Para 102].

In contrast the fact that "*economic common sense*" indicated that the claimant was involved in fraud was not sufficient [*Hussain v Hussain* [2012] EWCA Civ 1367].

Previous dishonesty

A witness' dishonesty in unrelated proceedings can be relevant for consideration of their credibility [*Shanley v Clydesdale Bank PLC* [2019] CSOH 75 at 33]. A witness' admission that they have previously been in dishonest in the context of the claim will also be relevant to their credibility as a whole [*Gilmour v Linea Directa Aseguradora Sa Compania De Seguros Y Reaseguros* [2017] SC EDIN 81 p20, and *Leander CB Consultants Limited T/A Leandor Advisors v Bogside Investments Limited, Alan Carson Mcleish* [2024] CSOH 09 at para 1].

Strength of contradictory evidence?

Even where the court rejects the submission that a witness has sought to deliberately mislead with their evidence, the evidence may be rejected on the basis what while honestly given, it is not reliable [*Prescott v University of St Andrews* [2016] CSOH 3].

Vagueness in the witness' evidence in general, when contrasted with a detailed recollection of pertinent facts may not be enough, similarly, inconsistency between the evidence given at proof and the version of events on record which amounted to a "*slight difference*" was not sufficient nor was apparent illogicity in the witness' actions, for example walking several steps in darkness to go to work after the accident rather than seeking medical attention [*Hill v Angus Council* [2023] SAC 9(Civ) 15.]

Differences, such as whether the front or back wheel of the pursuer's bicycle caught in tram tracks, or the precise location of her accident were "*insignificant*" when considered *"in the context of the short, compelling and coherent description of the accident"* given by the pursuer in evidence. It was also relevant that she was being asked to describe *"a brief event that occurred 5 ½ years earlier*" [*Elizabeth Fairley v Edinburgh Trams* [2019] CSOH 50 at p 170]

In ***Hill,*** the Sheriff was ultimately persuaded that inconsistencies between the pursuer's evidence at proof and the version of events recorded in the medical records were sufficient to conclude that the pursuer's evidence was neither credible nor reliable. These differences included saying in evidence he had fallen down stairs where that was not recorded in the medical notes, saying in evidence he had been brought to hospital by his father when the notes recorded that he had driven himself, and stating in evidence that he had been sent home from work early due to his injury, and the notes recording that he had worked a full day before coming to the minor injuries unit. It was significant in ***Hill*** that there were no other sources of evidence as to the accident circumstances against which to test the pursuer's evidence. The pursuer was therefore unable to prove his claim, and it failed. It is important to note that the dismissal of his case was not a consequence imposed as a sanction for deliberate dishonesty, but instead because the pursuer presented insufficient evidence to prove his case.

What needs to be in the pleadings to challenge a witness' version of events?

In Scotland personal injury actions are by default, managed in terms of **Chapter 36 in the Sheriff Court (OCR – Act of Sederunt (Sheriff Court Ordinary Cause Rules) 1993)** and **Chapter 43 (Rules of the Court of Session 1994)** in the Court of Session. These chapters set out a specialised personal injury procedure, characterised by standard timetables, mandatory valuations, and the use of abbreviated rather than full pleadings. Although it is possible for a personal injury action to be managed by different procedure, most often appropriate in cases where clinical negligence is alleged or other cases where fuller, more detailed pleadings are required, the majority of personal injury cases will follow the standard procedure.

Where a case proceeds in terms of the standard personal injury procedure, it is very unusual for the court to allow a debate, and a PBA is the default evidential hearing. That said, it does remain possible for a case to be irrelevant due to lack of specification, and so when fraud is suspected it can be difficult to determine what is required by way of pleadings. Notwithstanding the fact that "*elaborate pleading*" is not required, nor indeed considered desirable, it is necessary for parties to *"give at least fair notice of the case which it is proposed to make"* [*McGowan v W &JR Watson* (2007) SC 272 per Lord MacPhail at 278]

As what is being argued in this context is not substantive, rather the argument is that the pursuer's evidence should not be accepted because it is not sufficiently credible and reliable, and that therefore the pursuer has failed to prove their case, it is not strictly necessary to include pleadings to that effect. Indeed, it is not competent to plead evidence, nor to plead criticisms of the other party's evidence. [*Grubb v Finlay* [2017] CSOH 81 at para 12, and *Heather Capital Ltd (In Liquidation) v Levy & McRae, Heather Capital Ltd (In Liquidation) v Burness Paull* LLP [2017] CSIH 19], the purpose of pleadings is to set out the framework of the dispute, and the pleadings are not intended to allow the court to consider the merits of the evidence before proof, which would essentially be a "*trial by pleadings*" [Heather Capital, ibid per Lord Glennie p378]

However, there will be occasions where, in order to challenge a witness' version of events, it is necessary to present evidence of an alternative scenario, [*Robertson v Anderson* 2014 SLT 709]. It may be possible to cross examine a witness on the basis that the witness had provided a certain version of events themselves. In ***Robertson***, the defender was permitted to cross examine the pursuer to the effect that the conversation described by the pursuer in her evidence had been different, despite the fact that on record the defender simply denied that a conversation had taken place. This line of questioning was allowed because the pursuer offered in her pleadings to prove that there had been an agreement in a particular form [***Robertson v Anderson*** 2014 SLT 709 at 62] and the defender was entitled to test that.

Despite this possible flexibility, it would be best practice to plead any alternative version of events with which it is intended to challenge a witness in cross examination.

Do documents need to be disclosed and lodged in process ahead of proof?

It is not necessary for contradictory evidence to be lodged at court or flagged to the other party before it is relied upon; a document not previously lodged can be put to a witness during a proof or trial to test their credibility. [*Paterson & Sons (Camp Coffee) v Kit Coffee Co Ltd* (1908)16 SLT 180. And *O'Hare v Inverurie Skip Hire* [2019] CSOH 47]

In this regard, there is an important difference between documents relied upon as evidence to support a party's position and which *form "a substantive part of the party's case and documents which are used solely for the purposes of cross examination in order to test the credibility of a witness or to refresh his memory*". [*Paterson & Sons (Camp Coffee) v Kit Coffee Co Ltd* per Lord Salveson at 180]

Accordingly, while a party must lodge any document upon which they intend to rely to prove an averment, it is not necessary to call a witness to speak to documentary evidence relied upon to argue a prior inconsistent statement, for example where there is an inconsistent account in medical records [*Hill v Angus Council* [2023] SAC 9 (Civ) 15].

Surveillance evidence and related expert opinion need not be lodged immediately it is available, notwithstanding practice notes (in the Court of Session and the Sheriff Courts) requiring early disclosure [*O'Hare v Inverurie Skip Hire* [2019] CSOH 47.] This recognises the need for surveillance to be carried out without the pursuer's knowledge and "*over a reasonably substantial period of time*" and "*up to a point as close to the diet of proof as possible*" [Ibid, per Lord Bannatyne p25].

Do you need to challenge a witness to make submissions about credibility and reliability?

It is generally necessary to cross examine the witness with reference to a prior inconsistent statement in order for that statement to be admissible evidence with which to challenge the witness' credibility [Dawson v Dawson 1956 SLT 58 per Lord Walker and more recently Griffiths v TUI [2023] UKSC 48 as referred to in Ahmad v The Lord Advocate [2024] CSOH 54] However it has been noted that the failure to cross-examine does not put the trial judge "*into a straightjacket, dictating what evidence must be accepted and what must be rejected*" [*MBR Acres Ltd v McGivern* [2022] EWHC 2072 (QB) per Nicklin J at para 90].

When a challenge to credibility and reliability is made, there is no onus on the defender to prove an alternative version of events. If the pursuer cannot persuade the court that their version is correct, the pursuer's case must fail; it is not necessary for the court to determine what actually happened, nor why. The issue for the court is whether the pursuer has met the burden of proving what happened and why [*Ormsby v Chief Constable of Strathclyde Police* [2008] CSOH 143 at para 100]. However, where the pursuer's case fails because the pursuer has not discharged the burden of proof, there may not be a positive finding of fraudulent behaviour, the potential significance and consequences of that are considered in Chapter 5.

What does the court need to consider when arriving at a decision on credibility and reliability

The court must consider all of the evidence presented, including expert evidence, before arriving at a decision on credibility and reliability. [*Manley v McLeese* [2024] SAC Civ 16 at para 49]

Appealing first instance finding on credibility and reliability

In general, the appellate courts are very reluctant to revisit a first instance decision on the credibility and reliability of witnesses. The benefit of seeing and hearing the witnesses which is enjoyed by the first instance judge is such that their assessment of the evidence can generally only be questioned where it seems the judge has reached an irrational decision [*Thomas v Thomas* 1947 SC (HL) 45 more recently endorsed in *W v Greater Glasgow Health Board* [2017]]. This is not however a "*hard- and – fast*" rule [*W v Greater Glasgow Health Board* [2017] per Lady Dorrian at para 43]. Where what is challenged is an inference, rather than a finding of primary fact, the appellate court is more likely to be willing to reconsider the first instance finding [Ibid at para 44], on the basis that "*the intellectual process involved in drawing an inference of fact is liable to be less influenced by the judge's immediate perceptions of the witnesses*" [Ibid].

However, even where it was accepted that the Sheriff had erred in not considering all of the evidence presented a proof, the Sheriff Appeal Court did not believe that it could interfere with her decision on liability [*Manley v McLeese* [2024] SAC Civ 16 at para 52].

CHAPTER FOUR

AN ENTIRELY FRAUDULENT CASE

In Chapters Three and Four, the possible approaches to what might be considered, partially fraudulent, claims have been considered. However, there will be some cases which are entirely fraudulent. The obvious example is one which arises from an accident which never actually happened. In those circumstances a defender can ask the court to dismiss the entire claim.

Requirement for proof

It is unlikely that such a motion could be made without proof. The court will be reluctant to make a factual finding of dishonesty in the absence of proof, although it may be possible in "*rare cases*" [*Keenan v EUI Limited* [2020] CSOH 89 para 6]. The reason for that approach is because the court cannot "*subject the material to the kind of assessment and scrutiny which would have occurred after the hearing of witness testimony*" and the general "*difficulty faced by the court in attempting to reconstruct the outcome of a proof which never happened* [ibid at para 7] ***Keenan*** was a decision about the operation of the pre-QOCS rules on expenses in the context of a tender. However, the decision makes it clear that any motion to dismiss a claim because it is entirely fraudulent, is only ever likely to be successful if comes after evidence has been heard.

It is also important for such a finding to be made at proof, and the court is unlikely to be able to make the finding at a point thereafter.

[*Nicola Bruff v Royal and Sun Alliance Insurance Limited* [2024] SC EDIN 31 para 12].

The need for the evidence to be considered in its entirety was highlighted by the Sheriff Appeal Court ***in Manley v McLeese***, [[2024] SAC Civ 16] where it was found that the Sheriff at first instance had erred in considering only the evidence of the pursuer and defender in coming to her decision that the pursuer's evidence was incredible. That requirement was also highlighted in ***UK Insurance Limited v Gentry,*** where it was observed that, " *it is necessary to stand back and have regard to the whole of the evidence*" [[2018] EWHC 37 (QB) Per Teare J at P74]. This sentiment is echoed in the decision of Sheriff Campbell (in relation to the application of QOCS) where he commented that in considering whether there had been a fraudulent misrepresentation, it was necessary to consider the "*whole facts and circumstances of the litigation*"[*Gilchrist v Chief Constable Police of Scotland* [2023] SC EDIN 30].

Pleadings

As noted in Chapter 2, it is possible for the court to dismiss an action where the pursuer has failed to meet the burden of proof, however, that will not necessarily involve the court making a finding that the pursuer has been dishonest. At the conclusion of proof, in order to make the submission that the claim is entirely fraudulent and should be dismissed, the defender should have a positive factual averment that the claim is fraudulent.

There is an exception, where the fraudulent behaviour or representation occurs, or becomes apparent, in the course of proof. In those circumstances it is open to the court to find that a party is incredible and has made a fraudulent representation, even in the absence of an averment to that effect. This recognises that the basis for such a submission would only become apparent after the evidence has been heard [*Nelson v John Lewis* [2023] SC EDIN 44 at para 36].

In order to plead civil fraud in Scotland it is essential to aver that there was a false statement, made knowingly, with the intention to precipitate some action on the target of the fraud [*Leander CB Consultants Limited T/A Leandor Advisors v Bogside Investments Limited, Alan Carson Mcleish* [2023] CSOH 26] Without such averments, a defender will not have a competent basis for the submission that the claim has been brought fraudulently, this is subject to the exception above. There should be averments which specify what the representations were, when and where they were made, and in what way the representations provoked the target to take the relevant action, although the requirements may be less onerous in a personal injury action [*Royal Bank of Scotland v Holmes* 1999 S.L.T. 563].

In a personal injury action, the contentious points are most likely to be the false statement, and the knowledge that it was false at the time it was made; in the context of a claim for money brought against the defender, the motivation and attempted practical result should be straightforward to establish.

What constitutes fraud

An individual who is simply careless about the truth of what they say will not be found fraudulent [*Derry v Peek* (1889) 14 App. Cas 337 and *Robinson v National Bank of Scotland* 1916 SC (H.L.) 154]. It is necessary to prove, on the balance of probabilities, that there was a deliberate intention to mislead [*Gilchrist v Chief Constable Police Scotland* [2023] WLUK 646]. However, where the lack of care reaches the threshold of recklessness, then fraud may be established, this is so because someone who makes a statement not knowing whether or not it is true, in the knowledge that it will be relied upon by the court in reaching its decision, can be taken to have intentionally misled the court [*Nelson v John Lewis* [2023] SC EDIN 44 at para 35].

As discussed in Chapter 1, the Scottish courts have not dismissed cases as "*punishment*" for fraudulent behaviour. It is therefore necessary to aver and prove a fraudulent misrepresentation or misrepresentations which are connected with the validity of the claim itself. In order to secure dismissal of the pursuer's case, it is necessary to show that the entire claim is fraudulent and not simply that the pursuer has behaved fraudulently in some aspects of the claim.

As noted in Chapter 3, it is possible for a witness' evidence to be rejected as incorrect without a finding that the witness had deliberately sought to mislead the court. The defender must show that deliberate dishonesty is more likely than simple mistake. Where there are plausible reasons for a witness being mistaken, for example the passage of time [*Prescott v University of St Andrews* [2016] CSOH 3] or the age of the witness [*Lennox v Iceland Food* [2022] SC EDIN 42] or where some of the witness' evidence is consistent with other evidence [*Grubb v Finlay* 2017 CSOH 81] it will require strong evidence to establish that the witness has been deliberately dishonest.

Onus of proof

Although the onus is on the pursuer to prove their case, as previously noted, a finding that pursuer has been fraudulent does not necessarily follow the pursuer's failure to prove their case. If a defender wishes the court to find that the pursuer has been fraudulent, the onus is on the defender to prove that at proof. [*Khan v AXA Insurance PLC* [2024] SC EDIN18], this is because there is an assumption of honesty.

Sufficiency of evidence

Fraud must be the most credible explanation for the accepted evidence [Civil Fraud Law, Practice and Procedure 1st Edition, 34-072 and *UK Insurance Limited v Gentry* [2018] EWHC 37 (QB) "Per Teare J at P74]. The test is a high one, and in Gentry the judge formulated it as reaching a level which excluded the "*a real and substantial possibility that the accident was genuine*".

Where there are other plausible explanations which do not involve fraud, fraud should not be found proven [*Hussain v Hussain* [2012] EWCA Civ 1367]. In Hussain, the Court of Appeal found that there could not be a finding of fraud, simply on the basis that fraud was consistent with "*Economic common sense*" and that there was no reference to the accident in the claimant's medical records. That is, fraud must be more than plausible, it must be more plausible than any other possibility.

In any case, the court must carry out a balancing exercise and provide the basis for its decision. [*Hussain v Hussain* [2012] EWCA Civ 1367]. Although the facts which are relied upon may only be circumstantial, they must be "*sufficient in aggregate to tilt the balance in favour of a finding of fraud*" [Civil Fraud Law, Practice and Procedure 1st Edition, 34-073]

In ***Khan***, the pursuer claimed that he had been a passenger in a vehicle which had been struck by a second vehicle and had suffered injury as a result. After proof, the sheriff found that the accident had been deliberate, and that the pursuer, second defender (driver of the second vehicle) and two others had conspired to commit an insurance fraud.

In ***Khan***, the accounts of all witnesses, including the pursuer and defender were found to be incredible and unreliable. In reaching the decision that the claim was fraudulent, the sheriff relied upon the inconsistencies between the witnesses, the inherent improbability of some of what was said, and the lack of any other objective or reliable evidence with which to confirm what was being said.

Summary

Cases where the defender is able to prove that the entire claim was fraudulent are rare. It is important to recognise that the defender must go further than simply persuading the court that the pursuer's case is not likely on a balance of probabilities. A defender must prove that it is more likely than not that the pursuer has been deliberately dishonest with the intention of influencing the outcome of the case. Where there are other plausible explanations for the pursuer, or their witnesses, giving inaccurate evidence it will be difficult for a defender to meet this requirement; they must overcome the assumption of honesty.

CHAPTER FIVE

EXPENSES AND QOCS

Even where the court determines that the pursuer has suffered a genuine loss which should be compensated, it is open to the court to impose a sanction in expenses.

For example, in **Grubb,** although the pursuer was awarded some damages, he was found liable to the defender in expenses, restricted to two thirds of the total amount. This award was imposed as a mark of disapproval at the *"significant lack of candour"* with which the pursuer had advanced his case and prolonged the proceedings. The fact that the award was restricted reflected the defender's failure to prove all of its case on record and the fact that the pursuer had successfully established liability and some degree of injury. The approach is consistent with the requirement for a practical impact of the dishonesty, and that the court's actions should reflect that.

The extent to which this type of sanction is currently possible is restricted in personal injury cases by Qualified One way Costs Shifting (QOCS) introduced in Scotland in June 2021 by the **Civil Litigation (Expenses and Group Proceedings) (Scotland) Act 2018.**

QOCS

S8 of the 2018 Act introduces QOCS to personal injury actions and those for damages arising from the death of a person from personal injuries. It provides that the court must not award expenses against the pursuer in such an action, including any appeal in relation to the claim. However, that requirement only applies to actions which are conducted in an appropriate manner [s8(1)(b)].

In terms of s8(4) an action is not conducted in an appropriate manner if the pursuer (or their representative)

(a) Makes a fraudulent misrepresentation or otherwise acts fraudulently in connection with the claim or proceedings.

(b) Behaves in a manner which is manifestly unreasonable in connection with the claim or proceedings

(c) Otherwise conducts the proceedings in a manner which the court considers amounts to an abuse of process.

The 2018 Act is supplemented by **The Act of Sederunt (Qualified One-Way Costs Shifting) 2021** which brings the Act into force in relation to QOCS and provides more detail as to the operation of the rules. However, for our purposes S8(4)(a) of the 2018 Act is the most relevant provision. What is, and should be, required to satisfy that test was the subject of parliamentary debate before the Act passed and has been the subject of litigation since it came into force.

In order to understand what was intended and the current position, it is necessary first to consider the background to the 2018 Act and the wording of S8(4)(a).

Background

It was announced on 4 March 2011 that Sheriff Principal Taylor had been asked to carry out a review of the costs and funding of civil litigation in Scotland. This review was initially intended to form part of Lord Gill's **Scottish Civil Courts Review**, September 2009, but in light of Lord Justice Jackson's review of costs in England and Wales [Review of Civil Litigation Costs, December 2009], and the sheer scale of the task, Sheriff Principal Taylor's review was carried out and presented separately

Sheriff Principal Taylor presented his report, **Review of Expenses and Funding of Civil Litigation in Scotland** to the Scottish Government in 2013.

It is relevant for the purposes of this book to note that, in his forward, Sheriff Principal Taylor advised that although he had referred to Lord Justice Jackson's review this was for "*contextual purposes*" and that any similarities or differences between the Scottish and English and Welsh systems *"may be purely coincidental"* [Forward at i]. There was no intention to import the same system as had been implemented in England and Wales to Scotland. Indeed, in recommending that QOCS be introduced to Scotland, Sheriff Principal Taylor commented that he had done so for "*different reasons*" [Chapter 8, para 43] than those which had caused Lord Justice Jackson to recommend the introduction of QOCS in England and Wales

The motivation for introducing QOCS in Scotland was to promote "*equality of arms*" [Chapter 8 para 4] and to allow better access to justice for pursuers.

Although it was recognised by those responding to the consultation that it was necessary for there to be some circumstances in which QOCS was disapplied, there was concern that if the exceptions were not sufficiently tightly drawn there would be *"satellite litigation"* and that the resulting uncertainty would leave pursuers likely to seek reassurance by After The Event (ATE) insurance notwithstanding the introduction of QPCS [Chapter 8 para 24].

QOCS – exception for fraud

Sheriff Principal Taylor's recommendations

Sheriff Principal Taylor recognised that fraud on the part of the pursuer was a circumstance in which it would not be equitable for QOCS to apply. He discounted the approach taken in England and Wales whereby QOCS was to be disapplied where a claim was found to be "fundamentally dishonest" [Chapter 8 para 73]. Instead, he recommended that QOCS be disapplied where there had been "*fraud on the part of the pursuer*".

He referred to the definition of both fraud and fraudulent representation found in Scottish case law [Chapter 8 para 74 and see Chapter One of this book] he also highlighted the difficulty in distinguishing between a pursuer who is incredible and one who is simply unreliable [See Chapter 2 of this book]. For that reason, he did not believe that a finding that a pursuer is incredible should be sufficient by itself to disapply QOCS [Chapter 8 para 74]. This may reflect a quantitative requirement, that there must be a sufficient amount or gravity of dishonesty, or alternatively it might simply reflect the practical difficulty created by the common conflation of unreliability and incredibility.

Civil Litigation (Expenses and Group Proceedings) (Scotland) Act 2018.

When the Bill was presented to parliament S8(4)(a) referred only to a fraudulent misrepresentation, and not also to a pursuer who "*otherwise acts fraudulently in connection with the claim or proceedings*" as appears in the Act. The addition of this second scenario followed evidence to, and discussion at, the Justice Committee, and debate in the Scottish Parliament.

When he gave evidence to the Justice Committee on 31 October 2017 [Official Report, Justice Committee 31 October 2017; c11.] Sheriff Principal Taylor advised that fraud can be committed both "*by mouth*" and also by action. He was perhaps alluding to the expansive nature of the classic definition of fraud, insofar as the means by which it is perpetrated are concerned.

There were competing concerns raised by the MSPs scrutinising the bill; on the one hand, a desire that the protection of QOCS was retained, even where some inaccurate information had been provided and, on the other, a desire to provide meaningful protection for defenders against fraudulent claims. It was also recognised, with reference to Sheriff Principal Taylor's evidence, that behaviour before litigation was commenced should be included.

Ultimately, accepting Sheriff Principal Taylor's recommendations, it was agreed that "*fraudulent*" where it appeared in the 2018 Act should be defined in line with the Scottish legal definition of fraud, *"a machination or contrivance to deceive"* [Erskine Inst, III,I,16]. It was argued therefore that an innocent or isolated example of minor exaggeration would not be considered fraud, because that would not *"come close to fraud as it is defined in Scots law"*.

At the same time, it was specifically asserted that reference to dishonesty "*lowers rather than raises the bar required*" for QOCS to be disapplied [Annabelle Ewing, 26 April 2018]. These comments emphasise the requirement that someone must intend, not only to deceive by their dishonesty, but also to bring about a practical result.

It is clear that the exception was intended only to apply in the unusual case where the pursuer had made deliberate efforts to materially mislead the court as to the nature and/or extent of their claim. It was not intended to be relied upon on every occasion that a pursuer was found not to have been entirely honest, or where a pursuer's evidence was considered unconvincing.

Case law

S8(4)

There have now been several decisions which consider this sub-section.

General principles

From the early decisions which considered S8(4) it has been possible to discern some general principles which were summarised in ***Murray v Myktyn*** [2023] **SC EDIN 32** and have been repeated in several decisions since, the summary was recently approved by the Sheriff Appeal Court in ***Manly v Mcleese*** [2024] SAC(civ) 16 at para 55.

> *"(a) Each case in which the issue of disapplying QOCS arises must be considered on its own facts and circumstances (Lennox, para [61]; Gilchrist, para [26]).*
>
> *(b) 'Manifestly unreasonable' means 'obviously unreasonable' (Lennox, para [60]).*
>
> *(c) The legislative history and language indicates that the circumstances where proceedings were not conducted in an appropriate manner are likely to be exceptional (Lennox, para [61]).*
>
> *(d) Where there is a finding that the pursuer is incredible on a core issue in the action, the issue of manifestly unreasonable conduct may arise, but does not invariably arise (Gilchrist, para [26]).*

> (e) *The court preferring the defender's witnesses over the pursuer's account does not of itself give rise to disapplication; whether it does depends on the court's reasons (Gilchrist, para [27]).*
>
> (f) *Unusual circumstances may or may not be exceptional; whether they are is context-specific (Love, paras [56] & [65])."*

It is clear, in line with comments when the Act was passed, that while each case will turn on its own facts and circumstances, the cases in which QOCS will be disapplied will be exceptional and that the bar for justifying disapplication is high *[Murray v Myktyn* [2023] SC EDIN 32 and *Lennox v Iceland Food Limited* 2023 S.L.T. (Sh Ct) 73]

S8(4)(a)

Requirement for a finding of fraudulent misrepresentation

The approach to the threshold imposed by S8(4)(a) has also been consistent. It is necessary for court to make a finding that the pursuer has intended to deliberately mislead the court [*Manley v McLeese* [2024] SAC (Civ) 16 at para 58, *Gilchrist v Chief Constable Police Scotland* [2023] WLUK 646 at para 24, *Nelson v John Lewis* [2023] SC EDIN 44 at para 34, *Musialowska v Zurich Insurance* PLC [2023] EC EDIN 36 at 17A, *Mujahid Ali & Talib Hussain v Royal and Sun Alliance Insurance Limited* [2023] SC EDIN 35].

It is not possible to ask the court to make the finding after proof, even where there might have been other findings from which it could be inferred that the pursuer had sought to deliberately mislead the court [*Nicola Bruff v Royal and Sun Alliance Insurance Limited* [2024] SC EDIN 31] In ***Bruff***, the pursuer had relied upon a witness statement which she ultimately admitted she knew to be false. This admission came before proof, and on that basis, it was argued that it while it was not appropriate to make a finding of a deliberate intention to mislead at proof, there had been behaviour which met the S8(4)(a) threshold. In any event, the Sheriff did also find that the evidence given by the pursuer and her witnesses at proof was neither credible nor reliable. Significantly, he did not however make a finding that the pursuer had made a fraudulent misrepresentation.

At a hearing on expenses, the defender asked Sheriff Campbell to rely upon the evidence lead and submissions made at proof in order to make the finding that there had been a fraudulent misrepresentation. However, Sheriff Campbell was ultimately unable to take that approach and observed that "*the better view is that the court requires to proceed on findings in fact actually made, at least where the court is being invited to consider the issue after proof*".

This decision is a stark illustration of the importance of obtaining the specific finding of fraudulent misrepresentation. In ***Bruff,*** Sheriff Campbell rejected the evidence of the pursuer and her witnesses on the basis that they had been dishonest, in material respects, with the aim of influencing the outcome of the case; behaviour which would have satisfied the requirements for the finding.

It was also noted that the defender had made "*detailed submissions*" about the prior reliance on the fraudulent statement, which behaviour may also have satisfied the requirement for a finding of fraudulent misrepresentation. It is not clear from Sheriff Campbell's decision, after proof, nor at the hearing on expenses, why such a finding was not sought.

What is required to satisfy the court that the pursuer has been intentionally dishonest?

It has been observed that that "*fraudulent representation*" and "*acts fraudulently*" are not "*new legal concepts*". *Natalia Musialowska v Zurich Insurance PLC* [2023] EC EDIN 36 at para 13] and that the "*threshold for fraudulent misrepresentation is a high one*"[*Gilchrist v Chief Constable Police Scotland* [2023] SC EDIN 30 para 24] and see also *Manley v McLeese* [2024] SAC (Civ) 16 at para 59]. This is consistent with the discussion of the exception when the bill was passing through parliament.

It is important therefore to be mindful of the distinction between a witness whose evidence is unreliable and one whose evidence is incredible.

A simple finding that the defender's evidence is more persuasive than the pursuer's will not be sufficient to meet the "*high threshold or S8(4)(a)*" there must be a finding that the pursuer's evidence was deliberately untrue, or that they were incredible (rather than merely unreliable). Neither is it sufficient that the court has rejected the pursuer's evidence on a "*central plank of the case*"; it is the element of deliberate behaviour which is key [*Gilchrist v Chief Constable Police Scotland* [2023] WLUK 646 at para 24].

In ***Nelson***, the pursuer's evidence that he suffered hearing loss after a blow to his head, was rejected because his medical records disclosed that he had reported the hearing loss the day before the accident. However, it was also found that he had been consistent in his (albeit mistaken) account and that he had not sought to be deliberately dishonest. [*Nelson v John Lewis* [SC EDIN 44].

In ***Murray v Myktyn*** [[2023] SC EDIN 32] the sheriff found that although he couldn't be sure about the reliability of the pursuer's evidence, due to her narcolepsy, the issues arose from matters external to her evidence and he had no concerns about the pursuer's credibility, therefore the threshold for S8(4)(a) was not met.

In ***Manley v McLeese*** [[2024] SAC (Civ) 16] it was found on appeal that the pursuer was not reliable about her psychological symptoms relating to the accident, but she had not sought to deliberately misled the court "*At best she had forgotten for how long symptoms lasted. At worst she had exaggerated her claim*"[para 60]. It was also found that "*Being aggressive and swearing following an accident in which one's child is involved would not be unexpected The taking of photographs following a collision is usual practice*" [para 62].

By contrast, in ***Natalia Musialowska v Zurich Insurance PLC*** [[2023] EC EDIN 36 at 17] Sheriff Keir found after proof that neither the pursuer nor her witness could be considered credible or reliable, that their "*evidence contained significant inconsistencies*" and they had been "*evasive and defensive*" in cross examination.

For example, the pursuer's evidence was inconsistent with images of the vehicle damage, her evidence of absence from work was inconsistent with her employer's attendance records, and neither witness could demonstrate the mechanics of the accident with toy cars when they attempted to so in court. The pursuer did not lodge documentary evidence which she had claimed in evidence at proof would support her position and claimed, without any evidence, that documents and images lodged in court were incorrect or had been deliberately altered.

Sheriff Keir described the pursuer as "*a wholly incredible witness*" [para 22]. Significantly he commented that the issues with her evidence "*went far beyond the more common scenario where there are competing version of events, and the court has preferred one version over another*". Sheriff Keir formulated the test for S8(4)(a) thus "*on the balance of probabilities [the]] pursuer acted intentionally to mislead the court.*" [Para 23]

In findings similar to those in ***Musialowska***, in ***Mujahid Ali & Talib Hussain v Royal and Sun Alliance Insurance Limited*** [[2023] SC EDIN 35] Sheriff Keir concluded that the threshold for S8(4)(a) had been met, he found that neither pursuer was credible or reliable and that *"their evidence was peppered with significant inconsistencies and contradictions" [para 20].* He also observed, as he had done in ***Musialowska*** that "*The significant issues with their evidence went far beyond the more common scenario where there are competing versions of events, and the court has preferred one over the other*"[para 31].

In ***Ali*** the first pursuer provided unconvincing explanations for failing to take his car for assessment when a warning light came on after the collision, his evidence about the movement caused by the collision was contradicted by CCTV footage, his evidence about the damage to his vehicle was not supported by images lodged by him and which he claimed showed accident related damage and his claims to have sought medical attention for his injuries was contradicted by his GP records.

The second pursuer's evidence was equally problematic, Sheriff Keir described it as "*confusing and contradictory*" [para 25]. The second pursuer's evidence about the movement caused by the collision was also contradicted by the CCTV evidence, he said that he could see damage in the vehicle images lodged but no other witness had been able to identify any damage from the images, his evidence at proof contradicted a handwritten account of the accident he had given to his solicitor and his evidence at proof about the injuries he had suffered was contradicted by the contemporaneous medical records and his account to his expert medical witness.

These decisions are consistent with the requirement for the behaviour to be both deliberate, and directed at obtaining a practical outcome, in this context, influencing the outcome of the case.

Although the deliberate component of the dishonesty has been emphasised, someone who makes a statement recklessly, that is, not knowing whether or not is true, can be found to have made a fraudulent misrepresentation [Nelson at para 35]. There must be *"an honest belief in its truth"* [*Derry v Peek* (1889) 14 App Cas 337 at 375 per Lord Herschell]. Difficulties may arise in determining whether a belief that something was true was reasonably held, and observations in relation to reliability of evidence, where it has been accepted that the witness's evidence was incorrect, but the witness genuinely believed it as true, are likely to be relevant.

Practical points

There is no requirement for the defender to aver fraud in order to ask the court to make a finding that the pursuer has sought to deliberately mislead the court. This recognises the fact that the pursuer's dishonesty may not be apparent until the evidence has been heard at proof [*Nelson v John Lewis Plc* [2023] SC EDIN 44]. It is possible however that averments would be necessary to support a submission which refers to behaviour which was known to the defender before the proof.

An application to disapply QOCS must be made in a written motion [*Gilchrist v Chief Constable Police Scotland* [2023] SC EDIN 30 paras 4–5]

Summary

The bar for disapplication of QOCS is, by design, a high one. However, the approach taken by the courts in the decisions on S8(4)(a) to date, is consistent with the classic definition of fraud, and the authorities in relation to the credibility and reliability of witnesses.

It is now, following ***Manley***, clear that a specific finding that pursuer has made a fraudulent misrepresentation is required – and that this finding must be made at proof. Practitioners should bear this in mind when making submissions at the conclusion of proof. Although there is no requirement for an averment to support submissions which rely on behaviour at proof, where averments can be made before proof this is advisable.

CONCLUSION

As noted in the introduction, the Scottish definition of fraud, *"a machination or contrivance to deceive"* remains relevant and indeed, central, to the treatment of fraud in Scottish personal injury actions today.

Fraud must be deliberate, or reckless, not simply inadvertent or careless. It must also bring about a practical result; it must induce a practical outcome which would not otherwise have occurred.

There does not appear to be a basis in Scots law for the loss of a good civil claim as punishment for fraud. However, a claim can fail if the pursuer does not support their claim with credible and reliable evidence. It should be recognised however that unless there is a specific finding that a pursuer has been deliberately dishonest, then it will not be possible to rely upon the lack of success as evidence of a fraudulent misrepresentation.

In that regard, although the difference between credibility and reliability is not always clearly defined, the distinction can be crucial, and it is important to ensure that pleadings and the submissions made, reflect what is actually required. A finding that a claim is entirely fraudulent will be rare and the defender bears the evidential burden of proving that the behaviour has been deliberately dishonest with the intention of influencing the outcome of the case. The availability of another, equally plausible, explanation will undermine the argument that the claim is fraudulent.

The introduction of QOCS has resulted in a large number of decisions which consider what is needed to establish a fraudulent misrepresentation. Those decisions demonstrate that although QOCS itself is a novel innovation in Scots law, the principles underpinning the definition of fraudulent misrepresentation are not. It is clear that the 2018 has not created any new concept of fraud or fraudulent misrepresentation.

All of this simply serves to underline what was highlighted in the introduction, that the Scottish system offers various means by which to challenge and seek sanction for dishonest and fraudulent behaviour in personal injury actions, but in order to enjoy those opportunities, a practitioner must first properly understand the concept of civil fraud in Scotland and the procedural framework for personal injury actions.

Key to that is understanding the nature of the evidence available in the case. It may be that the evidence indicates a fabricated accident or that there was no injury whatsoever. More likely is that the evidence indicates a lack of truthfulness or reliability in the pursuer's reporting of the accident circumstances and/or the injuries suffered. If the evidence is of the latter kind, then it might not be possible to argue that the claim is entirely fraudulent, and any challenge will likely be restricted to the pursuer's credibility and reliability, with the reduced sanctions success on that basis would bring.

MORE BOOKS BY LAW BRIEF PUBLISHING

A selection of our other titles available now:-

'The Electronic Communications Code: A Practical Guide – Second Edition' by Kerry Bretherton KC, James Castle, Mark Loveday
'A Practical Guide to the Independent School Standards – September 2023 Edition' by Sarah McKimm
'A Practical Guide to Estate Administration and Crypto Assets' by Richard Marshall
'A Practical Guide to Parental Alienation in Private and Public Law Children Cases' by Sam King QC & Frankie Shama
'Contested Heritage – Removing Art from Land and Historic Buildings' by Richard Harwood QC, Catherine Dobson, David Sawtell
'The Limits of Separate Legal Personality: When Those Running a Company Can Be Held Personally Liable for Losses Caused to Third Parties Outside of the Company' by Dr Mike Wilkinson
'A Practical Guide to Transgender Law' by Robin Moira White & Nicola Newbegin
'A Practical Guide to 'Stranded Spouses' in Family Law' by Mani Singh Basi
'A Practical Guide to Residential Freehold Conveyancing' by Lorraine Richardson
'A Practical Guide to Pensions on Divorce for Lawyers' by Bryan Scant
'A Practical Guide to Challenging Sham Marriage Allegations in Immigration Law' by Priya Solanki
'A Practical Guide to Digital Communications Evidence in Criminal Law' by Sam Willis
'A Practical Guide to Legal Rights in Scotland' by Sarah-Jane Macdonald
'A Practical Guide to New Build Conveyancing' by Paul Sams & Rebecca East
'A Practical Guide to Inherited Wealth on Divorce' by Hayley Trim
'A Practical Guide to Practice Direction 12J and Domestic Abuse in Private Law Children Proceedings' by Rebecca Cross & Malvika Jaganmohan
'A Practical Guide to Confiscation and Restraint' by Narita Bahra QC, John Carl Townsend, David Winch
'A Practical Guide to the Law of Forests in Scotland' by Philip Buchan
'A Practical Guide to Health and Medical Cases in Immigration Law' by Rebecca Chapman & Miranda Butler
'A Practical Guide to Bad Character Evidence for Criminal Practitioners by Aparna Rao
'A Practical Guide to Extradition Law post-Brexit' by Myles Grandison et al
'A Practical Guide to Hoarding and Mental Health for Housing Lawyers' by Rachel Coyle

'Stephens on Contractual Indemnities' by Richard Stephens
'A Practical Guide to the EU Succession Regulation' by Richard Frimston
'A Practical Guide to Solicitor and Client Costs – Second Edition' by Robin Dunne
'Constructive Dismissal – Practice Pointers and Principles' by Benjimin Burgher
'A Practical Guide to Religion and Belief Discrimination Claims in the Workplace' by Kashif Ali
'A Practical Guide to the Law of Medical Treatment Decisions' by Ben Troke
'Fundamental Dishonesty and QOCS in Personal Injury Proceedings: Law and Practice' by Jake Rowley
'A Practical Guide to the Law in Relation to School Exclusions' by Charlotte Hadfield & Alice de Coverley
'A Practical Guide to Divorce for the Silver Separators' by Karin Walker
'The Right to be Forgotten – The Law and Practical Issues' by Melissa Stock
'A Practical Guide to Planning Law and Rights of Way in National Parks, the Broads and AONBs' by James Maurici QC, James Neill et al
'A Practical Guide to Election Law' by Tom Tabori
'A Practical Guide to the Law in Relation to Surrogacy' by Andrew Powell
'A Practical Guide to Claims Arising from Fatal Accidents – Second Edition' by James Patience
'A Practical Guide to Asbestos Claims' by Jonathan Owen & Gareth McAloon
'A Practical Guide to Stamp Duty Land Tax in England and Northern Ireland' by Suzanne O'Hara
'A Practical Guide to the Law of Farming Partnerships' by Philip Whitcomb
'A Practical Guide to the Law of Unlawful Eviction and Harassment – Second Edition' by Stephanie Lovegrove
'A Practical Guide to Costs in Personal Injury Claims – Second Edition' by Matthew Hoe
'A Practical Guide to the General Data Protection Regulation (GDPR) – Second Edition' by Keith Markham
'A Practical Guide to Working with Litigants in Person and McKenzie Friends in Family Cases' by Stuart Barlow
'Protecting Unregistered Brands: A Practical Guide to the Law of Passing Off' by Lorna Brazell
'A Practical Guide to Secondary Liability and Joint Enterprise Post-Jogee' by Joanne Cecil & James Mehigan

‘A Practical Guide to the Pre-Action RTA Claims Protocol for Personal Injury Lawyers’ by Antonia Ford

‘A Practical Guide to Neighbour Disputes and the Law’ by Alexander Walsh

‘A Practical Guide to Coercive Control for Legal Practitioners and Victims’ by Rachel Horman

‘A Practical Guide to the Law of Driverless Cars – Second Edition’

by Alex Glassbrook, Emma Northey & Scarlett Milligan

‘A Practical Guide to TOLATA Claims’ by Greg Williams

‘A Practical Guide to Elderly Law – Second Edition’ by Justin Patten

‘A Practical Guide to Responding to Housing Disrepair and Unfitness Claims’ by Iain Wightwick

‘A Practical Guide to the Law of Bullying and Harassment in the Workplace’ by Philip Hyland

‘How to Be a Freelance Solicitor: A Practical Guide to the SRA-Regulated Freelance Solicitor Model’ by Paul Bennett

‘A Practical Guide to Prison Injury Claims’ by Malcolm Johnson

‘A Practical Guide to Advising Clients at the Police Station’ by Colin Stephen McKeown-Beaumont

‘A Practical Guide to Antisocial Behaviour Injunctions – Second Edition’ by Iain Wightwick

‘Practical Mediation: A Guide for Mediators, Advocates, Advisers, Lawyers, and Students in Civil, Commercial, Business, Property, Workplace, and Employment Cases’ by Jonathan Dingle with John Sephton

‘The Mini-Pupillage Workbook’ by David Boyle

‘A Practical Guide to Crofting Law’ by Brian Inkster

‘A Practical Guide to the Law of Domain Names and Cybersquatting’ by Andrew Clemson

‘A Practical Guide to the Law of Gender Pay Gap Reporting’ by Harini Iyengar

‘NHS Whistleblowing and the Law’ by Joseph England

‘Employment Law and the Gig Economy’ by Nigel Mackay & Annie Powell

‘A Practical Guide to Noise Induced Hearing Loss (NIHL) Claims’ by Andrew Mckie, Ian Skeate, Gareth McAloon

‘An Introduction to Beauty Negligence Claims – A Practical Guide for the Personal Injury Practitioner’ by Greg Almond

‘Intercompany Agreements for Transfer Pricing Compliance’ by Paul Sutton

‘Zen and the Art of Mediation’ by Martin Plowman

‘A Practical Guide to Adoption for Family Lawyers’ by Graham Pegg

'A Practical Guide to Industrial Disease Claims' by Andrew Mckie & Ian Skeate
'A Practical Guide to Conducting a Sheriff Court Proof' by Andrew Stevenson
'A Practical Guide to Vicarious Liability' by Mariel Irvine
'A Practical Guide to Applications for Landlord's Consent and Variation of Leases' by Mark Shelton
'A Practical Guide to Relief from Sanctions Post-Mitchell and Denton' by Peter Causton
'A Practical Guide to Equity Release for Advisors' by Paul Sams
'A Practical Guide to Financial Services Claims' by Chris Hegarty
'A Practical Guide to Financial Ombudsman Service Claims' by Adam Temple & Robert Scrivenor
'A Practical Guide to Running Housing Disrepair and Cavity Wall Claims – Second Edition' by Andrew Mckie & Ian Skeate
'A Practical Guide to Holiday Sickness Claims – Second Edition' by Andrew Mckie & Ian Skeate
'Arguments and Tactics for Personal Injury and Clinical Negligence Claims' by Dorian Williams
'A Practical Guide to Drone Law' by Rufus Ballaster, Andrew Firman, Eleanor Clot
'On Experts: CPR35 for Lawyers and Experts' by David Boyle
'An Introduction to Personal Injury Law' by David Boyle

These books and more are available to order online direct from the publisher at www.lawbriefpublishing.com, where you can also read free sample chapters. For any queries, call us on 0844 587 2383 or email us at mail@lawbriefpublishing.com.

Our books are all generally in stock at www.amazon.co.uk with free next day delivery for Prime members, and at good legal bookshops such as Wildy & Sons.

We are regularly launching new books in our series of practical day-to-day practitioners' guides. Visit our website and join our free newsletter to be kept informed and to receive special offers, free chapters, etc.

You can also follow us on Twitter at www.twitter.com/lawbriefpub.

www.ingramcontent.com/pod-product-compliance
Lightning Source LLC
LaVergne TN
LVHW022315200926
848481LV00004B/1354
9781916698802